This book belongs to:

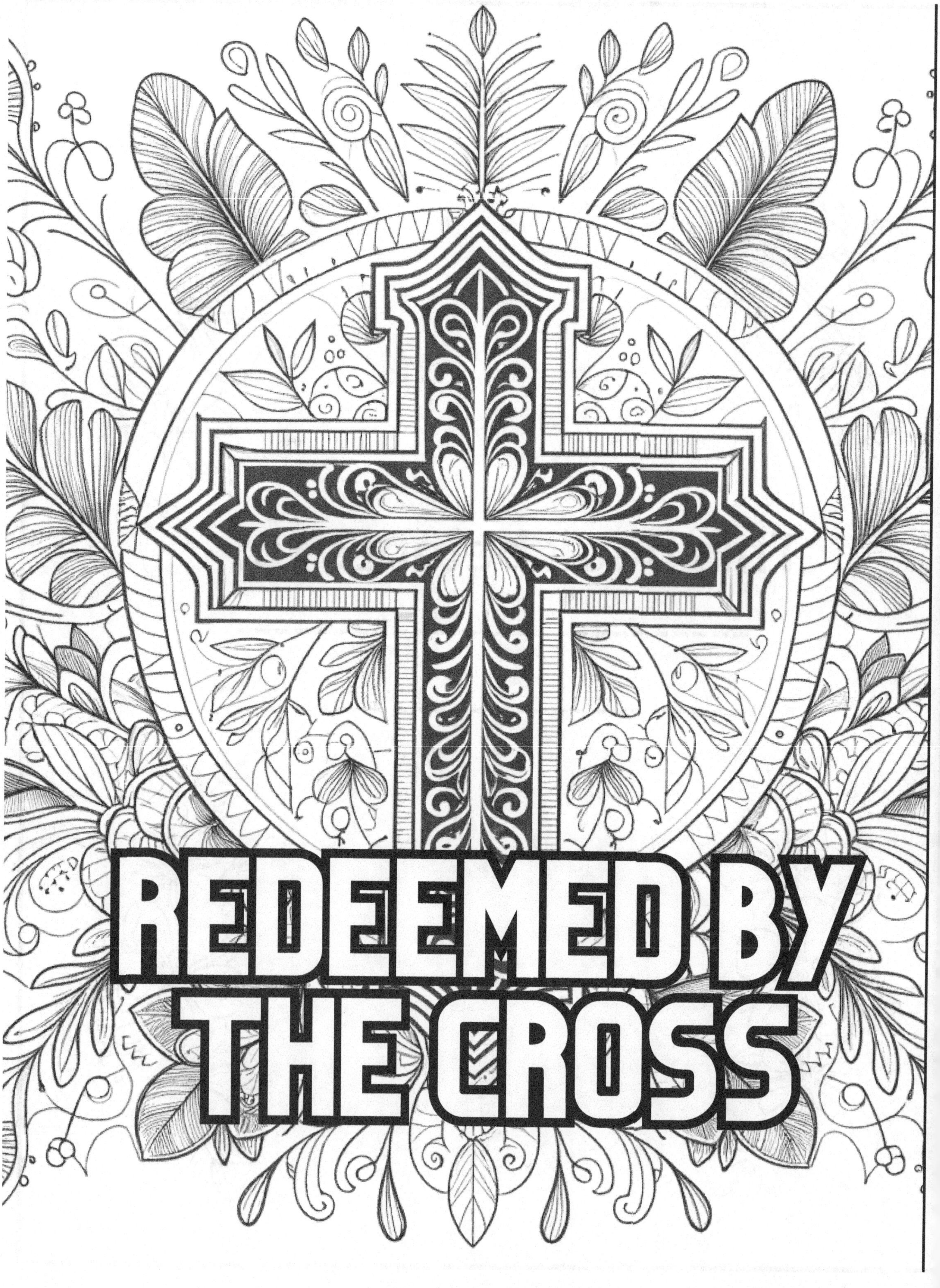
REDEEMED BY
THE CROSS

LOVE ENDURED
THE CROSS

INNOCENCE SACRIFICED FOR MANY

CHRIST'S LOVE
LIKE WATER

CLEANSING
FLOW OF
GRACE

DIVINE
PRESENCE,
ETERNAL
COMMUNION

NOURISHMENT
FOR THE SOUL

IN DARKNESS,
LIGHT SHINES

EMBRACING
LIGHT,
BANISHING
FEAR

THE TREE OF
REDEMPTION

THE LIFELINE
OF SALVATION

SYMBOL OF
HEAVENLY
GRACE

WINGS OF
FORGIVENESS
SPREAD

FLAMES OF DIVINE
TRANSFORMATION

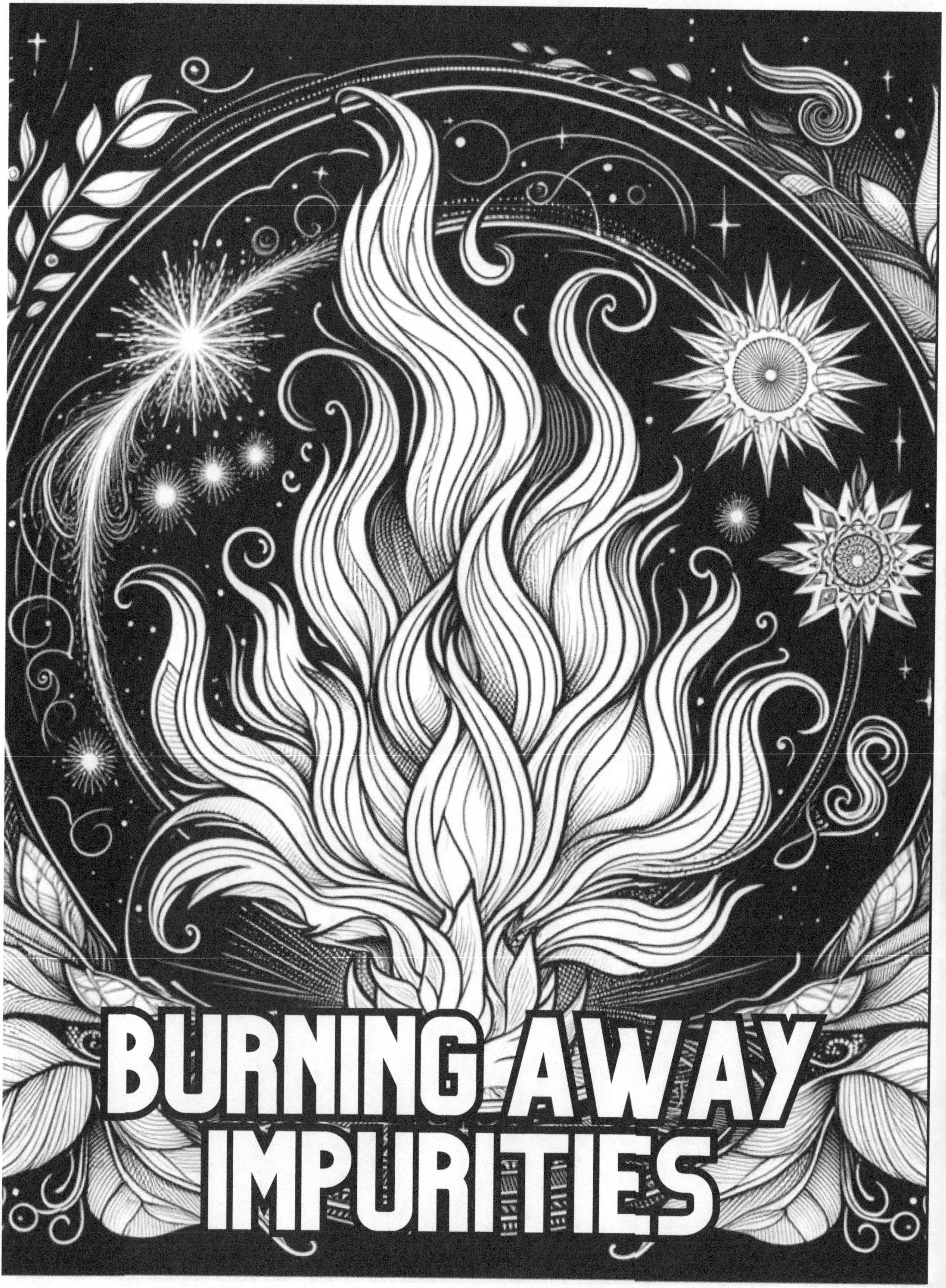
BURNING AWAY
IMPURITIES

TRIUMPH OVER
DARKNESS'S
DECEIT

CONQUERING
THE
SERPENT'S
LIES

NOURISHING SOULS
WITH LOVE

SYMBOL OF
FAITH'S
ABUNDANCE

GUIDING LIGHTS
OF HOPE

ILLUMINATING
PATHS TO
SALVATION

EMBRACING DIVINE COMPASSION

THE BEATING OF GRACE

THE ANCHOR'S
UNWAVERING
STRENGTH

ANCHORED IN
GOD'S LOVE

BEARING FRUITS
OF FAITH

BRANCHES
INTERTWINED IN
UNITY

BEAUTY IN DIVINE
CREATION

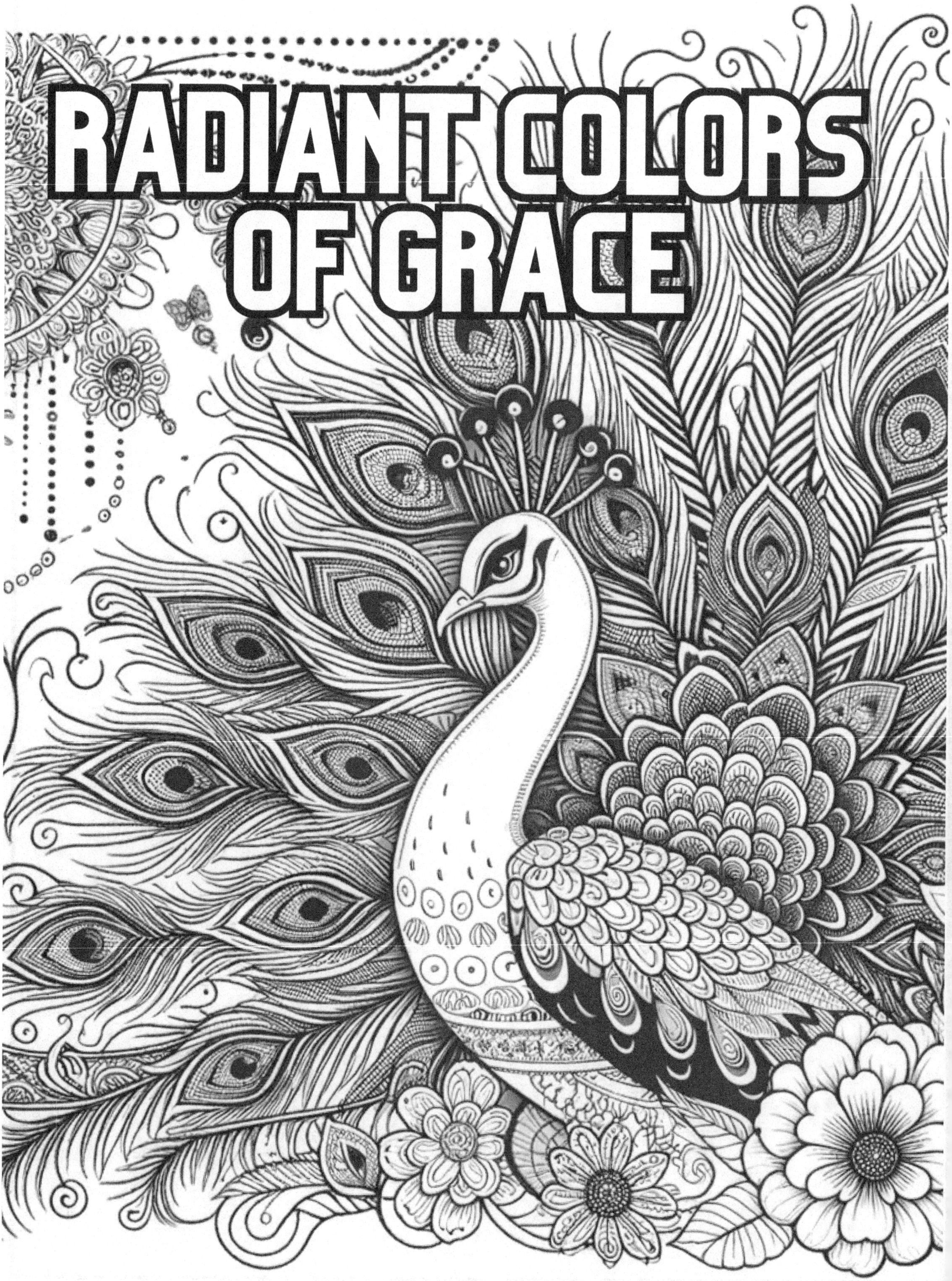
RADIANT COLORS
OF GRACE

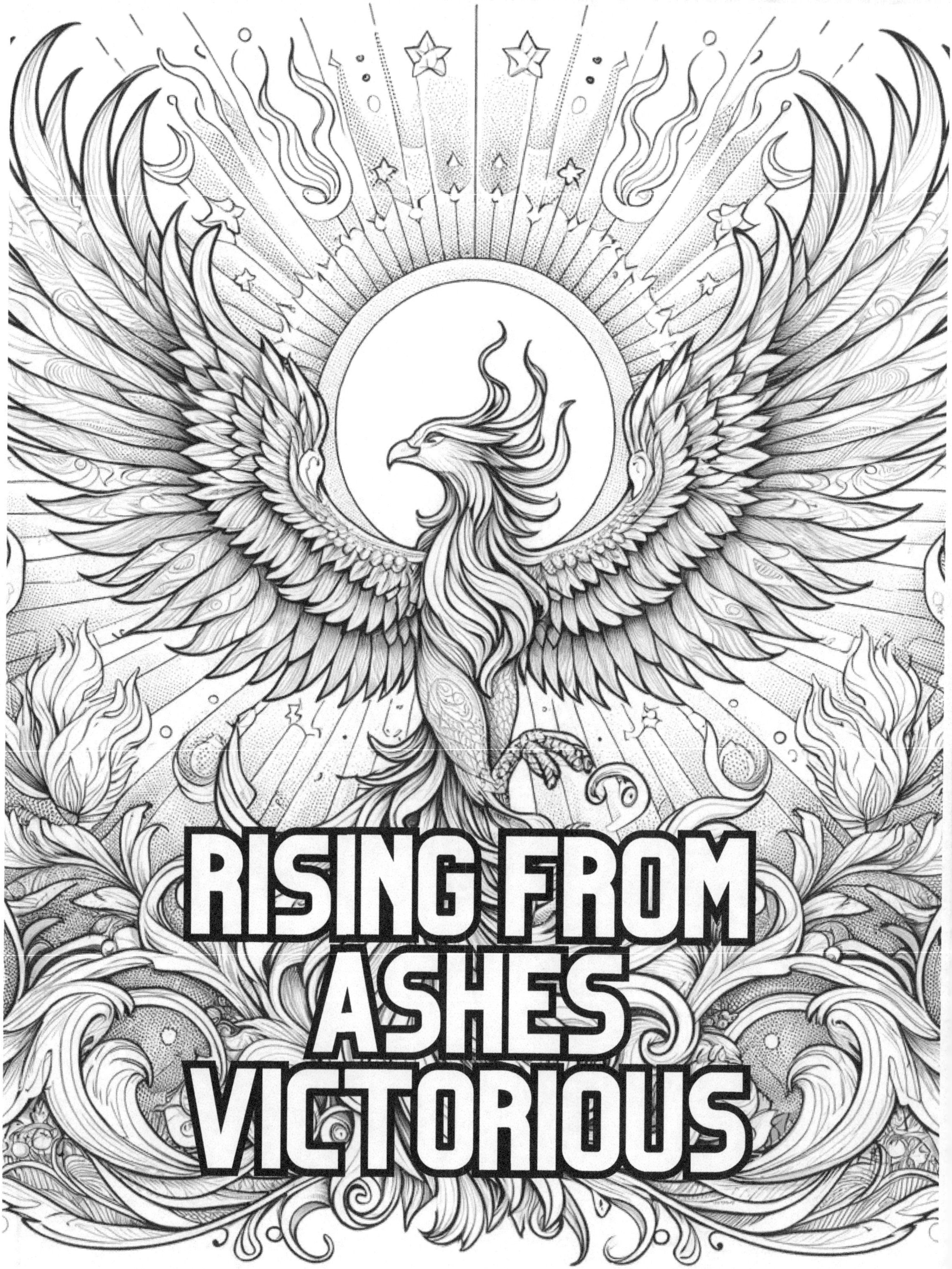
RISING FROM
ASHES
VICTORIOUS

RISING ABOVE
LIFE'S
CHALLENGES

BLOOMING IN GOD'S
LOVE

THE LILY'S
SACRED
ELEGANCE

Strength,
hope, &
Courage

Made in the USA
Columbia, SC
02 June 2024

36505867R00039